Basketball
Beyond the Bench

Aspire to be more than just a Player

Written by

Angela Fields

Illustrations by

Violeta Samson

ISBN: **978-1-7337020-1-0**
Printed in the United States of America

Illustrations by **Violeta Samson** (violetasamson.com)

Get Write Publishing
2770 Main Street-Suite 147
Frisco, TX 75033

To my Daughter Whitnie,
Thank you Whitnie for being my inspiration. I have always been your biggest fan throughout your basketball journey. You made me so proud when you became a Basketball Coach! I really appreciate all of the stories you've shared in your experience. Love you Always, Mom!

To my Mother,
Thank you Mom, through your eyes I love basketball just as much as you do. You are my hero, and I know your dream was to play basketball when you were younger. Because of your love for the game, I was truly inspired to encourage the younger generation to pursue their dreams. Love you Mommy!

To my Husband Mark,
Thank you Mark for being there throughout this process and being my rock. You always had by back and have been a shoulder to lean on when I face challenges.
Thank you for your love and support! Love you!!

To my Father,
You are my biggest supporter! Thank you so much for all of your love, encouraging words and prayers. You were always there for me to help me decide what to do.
I am forever grateful! Love you Daddy!

To my Son Travion,
Thank you so much for believing in me. I am so proud of your accomplishments in videography and throughout your career. I love and appreciate how you set goals for yourself and follow through until completion. Love you, my Resilient Travion!

To my Nephews and Nieces,
Thank you for letting me use your faces for some of the characters in my book. I pray that when you grow up this will inspire you to be successful and purse your dreams.
The sky is the limit. Love Auntie!!!

So you are interested in basketball? There are so many opportunities that your gifts can bring to basketball, beyond the bench.

Each person is born with unique talents. This is what makes you special. Basketball offers amazing jobs for athletes and non-athletes. Non-athletes are important people who work behind the scenes to make the game a success. Without their contributions, it will be impossible for the game to go on.

Throughout this book, we will explore various jobs that usually go unnoticed while watching the game.

2

4

Imagine that you are a famous basketball star. You have worked very hard for this moment. There are 3 seconds remaining on the clock. It all comes down to the last free-throw. You take a deep breath and remember all of your practices and training. Your team is counting on you to win the game…

Becoming a professional player takes hard work, dedication, and determination.

A lot of time is spent practicing the basic fundamentals such as dribbling, shooting, passing, lay-ups and rebounding.

It is important to maintain good grades in school by balancing time between homework, practices, and games.

A great basketball player displays sportsmanship and good character. That means someone who is willing to listen to instructions given by coaches, has a positive attitude, and is a team player.

The key to being an outstanding athlete is believing in yourself and your abilty to play. As a great player, what do you want people to remember about you?

You are the head coach of your team and all of your players are looking to you for guidance. You have to make a split-second decision during the timeout. "Ok guys we are down by 10 points, but we have to make better passes. Let's get the ball inside and get to the free throw line. We are doing good, but we have to play with confidence to get back into this game."

The coach is the leader of the team. He or she is responsible for motivating and teaching players the fundamentals of basketball. Some of the qualities of a good coach are leadership-skills, clear communication, and problem-solving abilities.

As a coach, you have to be knowledgeable about the game and develop practice drills for your players. If you became a coach, what would your coaching style be? Keep it simple, and have fun!

You are the lead referee officiating in an intense game between two rival teams. The home team shoots, but you notice the shooter is hit on the arm during the shot. You blow the whistle and everything stops. What call should you make?

A referee's job is extremely important. They are up close and personal with the players and action. Referees have the responsibility to control the flow of the game to ensure that it is safe, fair, and consistent. They are the ones who communicate the rules of the game to both the coaches and the players.

If a player is violating the rules, such as traveling or double dribbling, the referee's role is to immediately stop the game and make the right call. To become a great referee, a lot of time is put into training and learning the rules of basketball. As a referee, your main job is to stay focus and make good calls!

During the game, a loose-ball rolls on the floor. Players from both teams dive for the ball. "Tweet!" The referee blows the whistle, signaling a "tie-ball." One of the players gets up, but the other is still down holding his ankle. He is hurt. The athletic trainer knows just what to do. She grabs her medical bag and runs to his aid…

13

Sports provide opportunities for fun, fitness, and competitiveness. Your body is the most important part of physical activity. An athletic trainer's job is vital because they provide care for minor and serious injuries. Aid can be given to athletes before, during, and after games.

Before each game and practice, athletic trainers can wrap knees, shoulders and ankles to prevent injuries. If a player is hurt during a game, the trainer will treat the injury and determine if he or she can continue in the game. The number one goal as an athletic trainer is the safety of the players!

Behind the scenes, basketball managers work very hard. They are the backbone of the team. They help the coach and players during practices and games. At practices, coaches depend on managers to assist in preparation and drills.

On game day, the managers are responsible for packing and cleaning uniforms, organizing supplies, managing equipment, and recording stats. Other duties include providing water and towels for the players during the games. A basketball manager is always willing to assist the team with whatever they need!

It is game day and the players are in the locker room. As a basketball manager, you are responsible for setting up the gym by getting out the basketballs, towels and water. You check your list to make sure everything is ready because the coaches are counting on you!

16

You and your camera crew double-check the cameras for the last time. The game will be airing on live television in 5 minutes. You put on your headset to give directions on which camera angles to film. You zoom in and out to make sure the picture is clear. "Okay guys, we will be live in 5…4…3…2…"

The camera operator are the eyes of the game. They work hard to capture all of the action. Their job is very demanding because they must be attentive and focus on every moment of the game.

They must work as a team in different positions throughout the gym to capture the action on the court. It takes preparation and planning to film a live event. If we did not have cameras, how would we capture some of the greatest moments in sports history?

"Bongggg." The buzzer signaling half-time has sounded. The half-time show will be starting soon. There are hundreds of knobs on the soundboard in front of you, but you know exactly what to do. You adjust the controls of the microphone, so the sound can be heard clearly throughout the arena. When the lights dim, that is your cue to turn up the music and start the show…

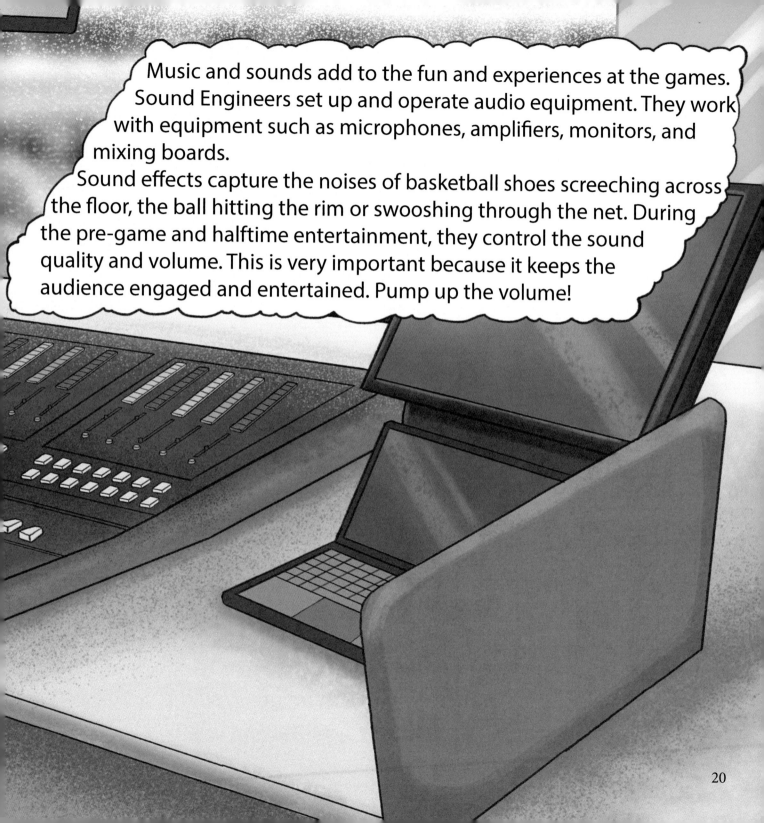

Music and sounds add to the fun and experiences at the games. Sound Engineers set up and operate audio equipment. They work with equipment such as microphones, amplifiers, monitors, and mixing boards.

Sound effects capture the noises of basketball shoes screeching across the floor, the ball hitting the rim or swooshing through the net. During the pre-game and halftime entertainment, they control the sound quality and volume. This is very important because it keeps the audience engaged and entertained. Pump up the volume!

The players have finished warming up, and are heading to the benches. You are the announcer about to introduce the starting lineups. You look over your scripts and player information sheets. It's game time! "Good evening, ladies and gentlemen! Welcome to tonight's matchup between the Bulldogs and the Wildcats..."

The announcer plays a major role in hosting the game. He or she communicates information to the audience. They introduce players, coaches, referees and the halftime performers. The announcer usually has a cheerful voice to keep the crowd excited.

They announce to the crowd when a player has scored, fouled or is at the free-throw line. During timeouts or at halftime, the announcer will share upcoming events or advertisements. Wouldn't it be awesome to welcome and entertain thousands of people?

A great commentator paints a picture with his or her words. Their expressions are animated and dramatic to keep the audience listening. They work for radio stations or television networks to report play-by-play action. It is not easy to keep up with such a fast-paced game!

However, the commentator does it with ease and confidence using excellent communication skills. The excitement in their voice can be heard when a player passes, dribbles, or scores. If you were a commentator, what would be your famous saying?

"We are back in action here in the 4th quarter. This has been a great matchup so far. It's all tied up with 5 minutes left on the clock. The Bulldogs inbound the ball to Jones, their point guard. The Wildcats are playing a full-court man-to-man defense. Jones dribbles up the court and passes to Young. Young drives into the paint; shot fakes, shoots… HE SCORES!"

"It's half-time, and it has been a battle so far in the first half. The zone defense has been working really well for the Bulldogs. They are making it hard for the Wildcats to score inside. Their shooting percentage has not been good tonight. They are only shooting 20% from the 3-point line…"

A sports analyst's job is to observe and report the performance of the game. To do their job successfully, they have to do a lot of homework! They study and gather information on the athletes, teams, and statistics.

Sports analysts give their opinions on game strategies, adjustments to be made, stats of players and discuss the team's strengths and weakness. They can work for news organizations, podcasts, radio stations or even magazines. Wouldn't it be amazing to work for a sports network where you are the expert analysis?

There are many jobs in basketball besides just being an athlete. Hopefully this book allows you to explore different options in basketball careers. Here are some points that will help you in anything you choose to do:

- Aim high
- Be a leader
- Work hard
- Get good grades in school
- Strive to be best you can be
- It's ok to be different
- Practice
- Set personal goals
- Don't be afraid to ask for help
- Don't give up

Most of all… be you!

About The Author

Angela Fields was born and raised in Saint Louis, Missouri. She grew up with a love for sports and attended many athletic games. After becoming a mother of two, her love for the games was passed onto her children. While attending her children's games, Angela began observing many facets that make any game possible. She was fascinated by the scores of people including coaches, commentators, sports analysts, videographers, and dozens more who make each game a reality.

This observation of the people behind the scenes, prompted her to share this information with the youth. Many children grow up wanting to be the star athlete and practice many hours, days and even years without achieving their dream. Being a member of a winning team is more than just watching star player. It includes hours of planning, coordinating the games, watching tapes of previous games, learning the strategies that make a team successful and much more. This understanding prompted Angela to write this book and introduce children to more than just being a star player on a team.

Throughout her life, Angela has accomplished many things as well. She coached her kid's Amateur Athletic Union (AAU) Saint Louis Blues Track Club. Angela graduated from The University of Missouri-Saint Louis with her Bachelors of Science in Accounting. Wanting to know more about the business aspect of any company, she earned her Master of Business Administration from The University of Phoenix. For the past 18 years, Angela, her husband and children have lived in Dallas, Texas. While writing her book, Angela became a Member of The Society of Children's Book Writers and Illustrators (SCBWI) in 2018. Knowing how important it is for children to aspire to be and do something great, Angela sat down and wrote Basketball: Beyond The Bench.

Made in the
USA
Lexington, KY